THE SACRED WEB

The magical craft of Your
Sacred Shamanic Space

ANGELL DEER

CONTENTS

INTRODUCTION

In an age where technology permeates every corner of our lives and the boundary between work and home blurs more each day, it is easy to become lost in the whirl of routines and responsibilities. The buzz of phones, the relentless pile of emails, the ceaseless chatter of social media, and the neon blinking of to-do lists can quickly overwhelm, leading to anxiety, stress, and spiritual disconnect.

The importance of striking a delicate balance between our outer demands and inner needs has never been more critical than it is today. Yet carving out some time for self-care, personal growth, and spiritual practice often take a backseat. It is reduced to the fringes of our lives - something many of us promise to do when we have a bit of spare time after fulfilling other commitments.

But in this continuous deferral of reconnecting with our inner selves, we miss the very essence of life and living. We start existing, not living. We become like hamsters on a wheel, always chasing, never arriving. It is merely surviving, not thriving. Our physical, mental, and spiritual well-being suffers. We create our depression, anxiety, burnouts, and dissatisfaction.

Over two decades has passed since I embarked on one of the most transformative journeys of my existence. This journey wasn't one trodden across the scenic landscapes of the globe, nor was it an exploration of exhilarating adventures.

Instead, it was a beautiful, introspective voyage that unfolded within my heart and the depths of my soul - the creation and nurturing of my sacred space. The deep remembering of my worth and purpose. The slow opening of a complete different vision of my life and the world.

Every individual who has ever stepped foot into my home upstate New York has shared with me that they felt a palpable shift in their consciousness, a resonance that hummed in their souls as they soften into the serenity infused in every corner of my dwelling. They marveled at the meticulously curated altar that reflected my spiritual practice, a shrine that stood as a testament to my unwavering dedication to inner growth and harmony. This is what inspired me to write this book and share my insights.

This evident aura of tranquility people felt not only from the altar but also into the entirety of my home and that melded harmoniously with the land upon which it stood, called many to explore this path with me. A piece of land affectionately named by the sacred white deer: "The Sanctuary," reflecting its deeply grounded spirit and the symbiotic sacredness it shared with everyone who walked this land.

This magical experience hasn't blossomed overnight. It symbolizes a patient pilgrimage spanning over two to three decades. It's a testament to the unflinching dedication that went into daily nurturing of this land and my heart. It is a mirror reflecting the profound spiritual work in the crucible of my being. And, it is an affirmation of the intimate bond between the land we inhabit, the inner work we commit to, and the sacred space we can create in our home.

In this guide, I extend an invitation for you to join me on a similar journey. A journey steering away from the incessant distractions of the modern world, towards a sacred haven nurturing tranquility, introspection, and personal growth; A journey transcending beyond the realms of aesthetic intricacies, to create an oasis of peace, a sanctuary for self-discovery, spiritual awakening and rejuvenation.

Regardless of your religious beliefs or spiritual inclinations, regardless of your knowledge of shamanism or animism, crafting a sacred space within your home has transformative potential. It serves as a keystone amidst the shifting sands of life, a beacon leading you back to your center, a reminder of the ethereal connection between you, your home, the land upon which it stands and the spirit world.

So, I invite you to join me in the Sacred Web of connections, through these pages, where we'll embark upon understanding the concept of a sacred space, its psychological and spiritual significance, and the enticing process of selecting, decorating, and nurturing your sanctuary.

Here's to hoping that at the end of this guide, you feel inspired and ready to elevate your home into a dwelling space for your heart, a refuge sculpted by serenity, and embark on a magnificent journey of self-discovery, introspection, and spiritual growth.

With my deepest gratitude to be walking this journey with you.

Angell

CHAPTER 1

WHAT IS A SACRED SPACE?

A sacred space, in its essence, is your personal sanctuary—a place dedicated to withdrawing from the exterior world's hustle and reconnecting with the tranquility within you.

Often mistaken as a religiously charged concept, a sacred space goes beyond the confines of religion or spirituality, and carefully embraces the breath of personal beliefs, spiritual practices, and aesthetic preferences.

At its core, it's a haven where you can retire, relax and recharge, a locus of peace and harmony you can always return to. A sacred space nestled within the comforts of your home bridges the frequently overlooked gap between outer obligations and inner well-being, and becomes an instrument of channeling clarity, creativity, tranquility, and spiritual alignment.

While it can be an entire room devoted to meditation, yoga, or other spiritual or personal growth practices, it could also be a quiet corner in your home adorned with objects that ground, connect and inspire you. It's where you start your morning with inspiration, engage with personal growth activities during the day, or unwind in the evening. It can be your refuge at anytime of heavy emotions or life troubles.

Irrespective of how and where you choose to create this space, it is essential that it reflects who you are and what you need - an extension of your essence. I did not want to write this book with just my personal views on shamanism, but open the possibility for everyone to find meaning and guidance in this writing.

So to be clear it does not need to have crystals or feather! Whether it's filled with books you enjoy, adorned with soothing art, scented with your favorite fragrances, lit up with soft candle flames or echoing with serene harmonies, a sacred space becomes your personal retreat from the world - a fortress safeguarding your peace in the bustling chaos of everyday life.

And it ultimately is a reflection of your most intimate and often unseen desires, dreams and prayers.

That said I do believe there is potentially a deeper power in following ancient teachings of one specific lineages, it is not something you might be call into. I will just share here that as I embraced the Andean Cosmovision teachings, prayers, altar and sacred space guidances, my practice went to a whole other level.

As we progress further, you will learn in more detail the potential ways you can create and utilize your sacred space for promoting self-care, personal growth, and spiritual advancement. From understanding its psychological significance to decorating it to resonate with your energy, we will explore the various facets of setting up and maintaining your sanctuary.

For each chapter I share the general information on the topic and added a specific "shamanic perspective" about it for those of you who wish to connect more deeply through those ancient lenses.

So let's start the weaving into the Sacred Web...

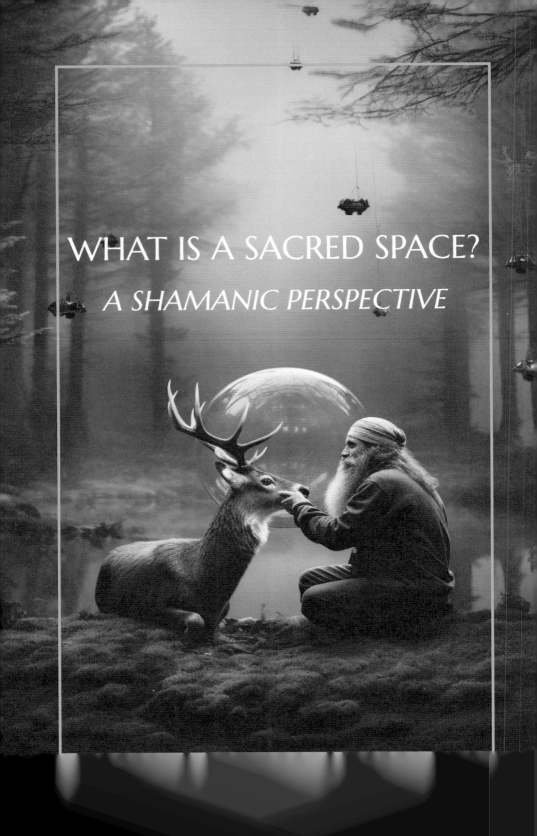

WHAT IS A SACRED SPACE?

A SHAMANIC PERSPECTIVE

"A shamanic perspective"

From a Shamanic practitioner's perspective, understanding a sacred space goes beyond the physical, extending into the spiritual realm and the elements of the Earth. Here, a sacred space is seen as a bridge between the physical world and the spiritual plane. Shamanic traditions view everything as imbued with spirit or life force, including the space around us.

For the Shamanic practitioner, a sacred space is an intersection of the elemental forces - where earth, air, fire, and water converge with the spirit world. They observe nature's sanctuaries - glades, caves, riverbanks, and mountain tops - as templates for their own sacred spaces, emulating the elemental harmony found there.

In setting a sacred space, a Shamanic practitioner seeks not just to create a physical environment for spiritual practices, but primarily to summon a microcosm of the greater cosmos as they perceive it. They invite the spirits, ancestors, and the elemental forces, making the space a bustling crossroad of energies, which can both be seen and unseen.

Hence, the sacred space becomes a personal cosmos, a mirror of the universe within one's own dwelling. This grounded yet transcendent view of a sacred space makes the Shamanic practitioner's perspective a deeply enriching one, adding layers of meaning and profundity to the concept of a sacred space.

CHAPTER 2

THE PSYCHOLOGICAL IMPORTANCE OF A SANCTUARY AT HOME

In the era of constant connectivity and fast-paced lifestyles, we're incessantly inundated with stimuli that draw us further from our inner selves and into the external world's chaos. As a result, we become more prone to feelings of stress, anxiety, and disconnection. In this context, the creation of a sanctuary at home arises as more than an opulent fad - it poses as a psychological lifeline.

This dedicated space serves as a physical reminder to slow down, retreat into a state of stillness, and reconnect with our very essence. It fosters a realm where we find solace from the ceaseless external noise and commune with our thoughts and feelings. Retreat into this sanctuary can pivot our focus inwards, stirring a mindful awareness of our emotional and mental states.

Returning to the familiar and peaceful environment of your sacred space after an arduous day imparts a sense of control and predictability, mitigating stress and anxiety. Such spaces, according to environmental psychology, can induce calm, helping us de-stress and recharge. The mere act of being in an environment that commands peace and tranquility has a soothing effect, akin to the tender embrace of nature.

Additionally, this sanctuary you create at home can play a pivotal role in habit formation. As per the science of neuroplasticity, our brains can change and adapt with repeated experiences. Consistently carving out time to retreat to your sacred space for self-care activities - be it yoga, meditating, journaling, reading, or practising gratitude - creates neural pathways that soon form a ritual. This ritual then reinforces positive habits, contributing to personal growth and inspiring a more fulfilling life experience.

Moreover, a sanctuary at home allows for introspection and self-reflection, which are vital for emotional intelligence and self-improvement. With such a nurturing environment at hand, the journey of personal growth and self-improvement becomes a process full of joy, serenity, and profound discoveries.

In the subsequent chapters, we will delve deeper into how to choose and create such a sanctuary within your homes, embracing the power it has to drastically improve mental wellness, drive personal growth and open your spiritual quest.

THE PSYCHOLOGICAL IMPORTANCE OF A SANCTUARY AT HOME

A SHAMANIC PERSPECTIVE

"A shamanic perspective"

In the view of a Shamanic practitioner, the concept of a sanctuary at home resonates beyond just a psychological level—it touches the spiritual and emotional realms too. Here, home becomes not only a physical dwelling but also a spiritual retreat. It's a place where the harmony of external surroundings aligns with inner tranquility. Shamanic practitioners surpass the traditional notion of home and elevate it to a sanctuary—a sacred space where they communicate with the spiritual realm and perform ancestral ceremonies. This sacred communion amplifies their spiritual practices, resulting in an enriched mental state and emotional well-being.

A sanctuary at home is seen by the Shamanic practitioner as a spiritual hub—a gateway into realms beyond the physical. This perspective ties into the psychological importance of a sanctuary at home, merely amplifying it by embracing the spirits, elements, ancestors, and natural rhythms that infuse the home with sacred significance. The essence of Shamanic tradition is about honoring interconnectedness with all life forces. Thus, the sanctity of the home sanctuary naturally aids in reducing stress, fostering mindfulness, and nurturing a sense of belonging. This is because, in this spiritually fortified domain, a Shamanic practitioner can delve into deeper introspection, gain insightful wisdom, and enhance the psychological equilibrium.

Hence, for a Shamanic practitioner, a sanctuary at home serves a dual purpose. While it bolsters psychological health through a strong emotional connection to the personal space, it also fosters a deeper spiritual connection with the greater cosmos, supplementing their psychological well-being with profound spiritual experiences.

CHAPTER 3

HOW TO CHOOSE A LOCATION FOR YOUR SACRED SPACE

The adoption of a special retreat within your home demands careful contemplation about where to create it. It requires a space that resonates with your energy, comforts your spirit, and provides undisturbed solace. The choice of location for your sacred space can be as unique as you are, and depends foremost on your personal preference and the physical layout of your living environment.

For some, a quiet corner swathed with morning sunlight brings peace, while for others, a cozy niche adorned with soft lights for evening prayers suits better. It could be an under-utilized attic, an outdoor garden, a secluded section of your living room or a specially designed meditation room. Irrespective of its size or grandeur, what truly matters is your identification with the space and the comfort you find there.

Here are a few considerations to keep in mind when selecting a location for your sacred space:

1. Quiet and Private:

Choose a location that offers reprieve from routine chaos and noise. Seek out an area that's less likely to invite interruptions, bestowing you with the privacy you need for introspection and concentrated focus on self-care and personal growth.

2. Natural Light and Ventilation:

Natural light often contributes to the enhancement of mood and energy levels. If possible, pick a location near a window where sunlight pours in, or that offers a soothing view of nature. Good ventilation is equally important to maintain air freshness.

3. Spaciousness:

Remember that your sacred space should be spacious enough for you to sit comfortably, and to accommodate any important objects or personal artifacts. It doesn't need to be an entire room; even a peaceful corner can be transformed into a sanctuary.

4. Positive Vibes:

Above all, the location should resonate with positive energy. It should be a place where you naturally feel good, calm, and at peace. Trust your gut feeling while pinpointing your sacred space. Do you feel relaxed and peaceful in your chosen location? If yes, you've found the perfect place.

After selecting the perfect location for your sanctuary, it's time to personalize it. Up next, we embark on the journey of decorating your sacred space, infusing it with thoughts, beliefs, prayers and objects tied closely to your soul.

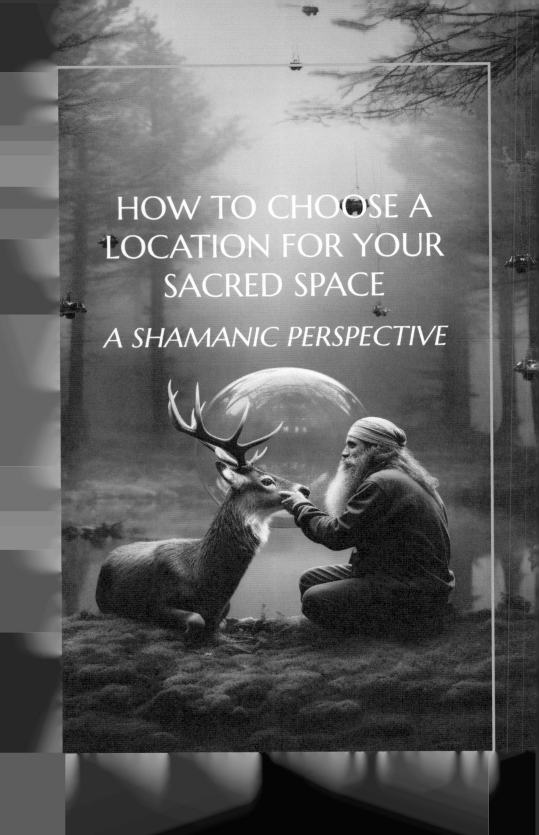

HOW TO CHOOSE A LOCATION FOR YOUR SACRED SPACE

A SHAMANIC PERSPECTIVE

"A shamanic perspective"

For a Shamanic practitioner, choosing a location for a sacred space extends beyond visible attributes to encompass energy vibrations and elemental balance, mirroring the ethereal amalgamation seen in natural sanctuaries.

They consider not just the physical characteristics of the space, like light, size, and silence, but also its energy, envisioned as the convergence of the elemental forces—earth, water, air, fire, and spirit. The goal is to replicate the energetic harmony found in nature within their home sanctuary.

A Shamanic practitioner may seek guidance from the spirit world in choosing a location, perhaps through a journeying ritual or through interpreting signs in the natural world. They perceive their sacred space as a resilient anchor to the spiritual realm even amidst their household. The chosen location should also ideally allow for ceremonial activities central to Shamanic practice like circle rituals, drumming, or dance. It should accommodate symbolic representations of elemental forces, like a bowl of earth or water, candles symbolizing fire, or feathers signifying air—as they enable a better connection with the spiritual plane.

In Shamanic practice, every direction—north, east, south, and west—hold specific significance. Thus, the location's orientation could be considered, aligning it, for instance, with the east for new beginnings or the west for introspection.

Therefore, in choosing a suitable location for their sacred space, Shamanic practitioners perceive it as a rendezvous of the earthly realm and the spiritual cosmos. This transcendent view brings added depth and inspiration to the process of choosing a location for your sacred space.

CHAPTER 4

DECORATING YOUR SACRED SPACE

blessings

Once you've identified an ideal location for your sanctuary, the next adventurous phase is decorating it. This process is highly personal and creativity-invoking. It's an opportunity to design a space in congruence with your energy, taste, and purpose. It's about manifesting a physical environment that brings you joy, peace and comfort.

An effective approach to cultivating tranquillity in your sanctuary is by incorporating elements of nature. Nature has a profound effect on our senses - it calms the mind, relaxes the body, and uplifts the spirit. Drawing inspiration from natural elements can significantly intensify the sacredness of your space.

Below are a few ideas to decorate your space using elements of nature:

1. Greenery:

Plants and flowers are simple yet powerful additions that emanate life and freshness in your sacred space. They not only improve air quality but also add a vibrant touch to your space. Considering adding peace lilies for their serene beauty or snake plants for their air-purifying abilities.

2. Natural Light:

Harness the power of natural light. If your space has access to a window or skylight, allow the sunlight to flood in. You could also use sheer draping to create a soft, diffused glow.

3. Water Element:

This could be as simple as a small tabletop fountain or go as far as an indoor koi pond, depending on space and budget. The soothing sounds of flowing water can have a remarkably calming effect, promoting relaxation and mindfulness.

4. Earth Elements:

Consider introducing earth elements like stones, crystals, or wood. They ground and balance the environment, often carrying symbolism that can enhance your sacred rituals or practices.

5. Incense or Essential Oils:

Scents are a powerful sensory stimulation, not just purifying the environment, but also setting an uplifting or calming mood. Using natural incense sticks or essential oils like lavender or sandalwood can make your sanctuary a rich sensory haven.

6. Natural Sounds:

Consider playing soft nature sounds such as the chirping of birds, rustling of leaves, or ocean waves. You could do this with a simple sound machine or smart speaker.

Remember, your sacred space must be a true reflection of your inner self and what you find comforting and inspiring. What matters most is that the space resonates with you on a deeper level and serves its purpose of providing tranquillity, fostering self-reflection, and promoting personal growth. The next section will look into the symbolism of particular objects in your space and how they might be significant to your spiritual practice or self-care rituals.

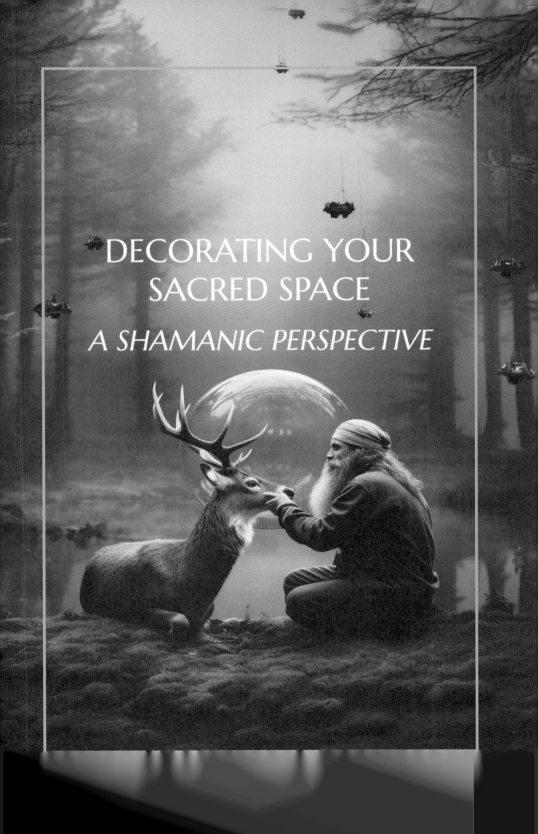

DECORATING YOUR SACRED SPACE

A SHAMANIC PERSPECTIVE

"A shamanic perspective"

Shamanic practitioners resonate deeply with the concept of incorporating elements of nature into their sacred spaces, given their reverence for the natural world and its connection to the spirit realm. To them, each element of nature is a doorway to the divine, a symbol of the great web of life.

Embracing the wisdom of nature, they incorporate in their sacred spaces elements such as stones, crystals, feathers, flowers, and water, attributing to each different energetic qualities and meanings. Stones and crystals may represent the grounding stability of earth, feathers the freedom of air, and water a symbol of emotional and spiritual cleansing.

A Shamanic practitioner may fill their sanctuary with shells for their affinity with the water element, housing a pot of soil or a hearty indoor plant that represents earth, or perhaps keeping a flame always alive to symbolize fire. Each element holds deep importance and is seen as a manifestation of a particular nature spirit.

Autumn leaves may be used during autumn to enforce an internal state of letting go, and fresh green leaves or flowers during spring to reinvigorate growth and rebirth. They arrange their sacred space to follow the cyclic rhythm of nature, mirroring the seasonal changes outside within their indoor sanctuaries.

Rather than using decorations for mere aesthetic appeal, a Shamanic practitioner sees them as living beings, teeming with the spirit and embodying profound symbolic meaning. Thus, in decorating their space, they celebrate the wonders of the natural world indoors and uphold a potent connection between their personal sacred space and the grander spirit-influenced universe.

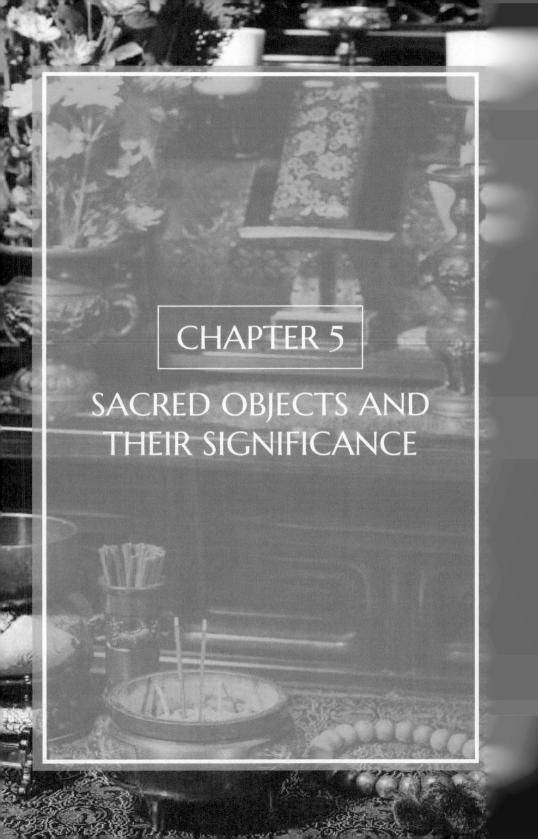

CHAPTER 5

SACRED OBJECTS AND THEIR SIGNIFICANCE

*S*acred objects, when incorporated in your personal sanctuary, add a deeper layer to your spiritual practice and personal growth journey. These objects not only adorn your space but infuse it with profound symbolism and a tangible connection to your spiritual and personal aspirations.

The significance of these items sparkles in the emotions and feelings they ignite within you – a sense of solace, the impulse of motivation, or a reminder of peace and self-care. Be intentional about what you include, ensuring each object resonates with your spiritual belief system or stimulates the state of mind you desire to foster in that space.

Here are some ideas of what you might consider bringing into your personal sanctuary:

1. Symbols of Faith:

Symbols, images or statues depicting your faith or belief system can add a spiritual essence to your sanctuary. They serve as a focal point for your spiritual practice and a reminder of your spiritual path.

> **Example:** Place a figurine, painting, or symbol representative of your faith. For example, if you follow Buddhism, a statue of the Buddha in a meditative pose can serve as a focal point in your sacred space.

2. Personal Memorabilia:

Photographs, letters, or any item with emotional value can make your sanctuary feel deeply personal. They can serve as reminders of loved ones, significant life events, or personal milestones reached.

> **Example:** Frame a touching handwritten letter from a loved one or display a photograph from a soul-stirring solo trip.

These memorabilia should trigger positive emotions and inspire introspection whenever you glance at them.

3. Inspirational Books:

A stack of thought-provoking or inspirational books can assist in fostering personal growth. Whether it's about mindfulness, philosophy, spirituality, or motivation, choose books that inspire and guide you.

> **Example:** Books can range from the philosophical teachings of Thich Nhat Hanh to the motivating narratives of your favorite author. Choose texts that invigorate your spirit and open avenues for personal growth.

4. Crystals and Stones:

Beyond their natural aesthetic appeal, different crystals and stones are believed to hold different energies and healing properties. Select those that resonate with your intentions for the space.

> **Example:** For someone aiming for calming energy in their sacred space, a rose quartz (often associated with love and gentleness) can be a lovely addition.

Alternatively, an Amethyst, known for its calming and meditative energy, can also be strikingly relevant.

5. Candles or Oil Lamps:

Candles cast a warm, calming glow, fostering a peaceful ambiance. Some may prefer oil lamps, as they have been an age-old element in various spiritual traditions.

> **Example:** Light a lavender-scented candle for a calming effect or a bright citrus one for an invigorating boost. If you

prefer an oil lamp, opting for oils that enhance focus like rosemary or clary-sage can uplift your spiritual practices.

6. Incense or Essential Oils:

Similar to candles, incense or diffused essential oils can create an inviting aroma that affects mood and evokes a sense of calmness.

Example: Burn sandalwood incense sticks to invoke a serene environment, or patchouli for grounding and balance. For essential oils, diffusing frankincense can be conducive to meditation, while lavender can create a calm atmosphere.

7. Journal:

A dedicated journal or notebook for recording your thoughts, emotions, affirmations, or sketching can be a valuable addition to your sanctuary.

Example: Keep a beautiful journal in your space, dedicated solely to your spiritual reflections. You might start entries with thought-provoking prompts like "Today, I discovered..." or "While meditating, I felt..."

8. Meditation Accessories:

Based on your practices, you might want to include a meditation cushion, mat, or mala beads in your sacred space.

Example: A meditation cushion or Zafu, in a beautiful deep teal tone, can induce calmness and add a touch of color to your space. Or consider choosing pure white mala beads made of clear quartz, which are often used to stimulate clarity in thoughts.

9. Wind Chimes or Bells:

Sound is a powerful component in many spiritual practices. Wind chimes, bells or singing bowls can be used to signify the beginning or the end of a ritual.

Example: Consider adding brass wind chimes to your space to capture the light, delicate notes of the wind, marking the start or end of your spiritual practice. Or, a Tibetan singing bowl, with its resonating sound, can be beneficial to ground one's attention during meditation.

As you populate your sanctuary with meaningful objects, it transforms into a tangible extension of your internal world. In the next chapter, we delve into how to maintain the sanctity of your space and keep its energies positively charged.

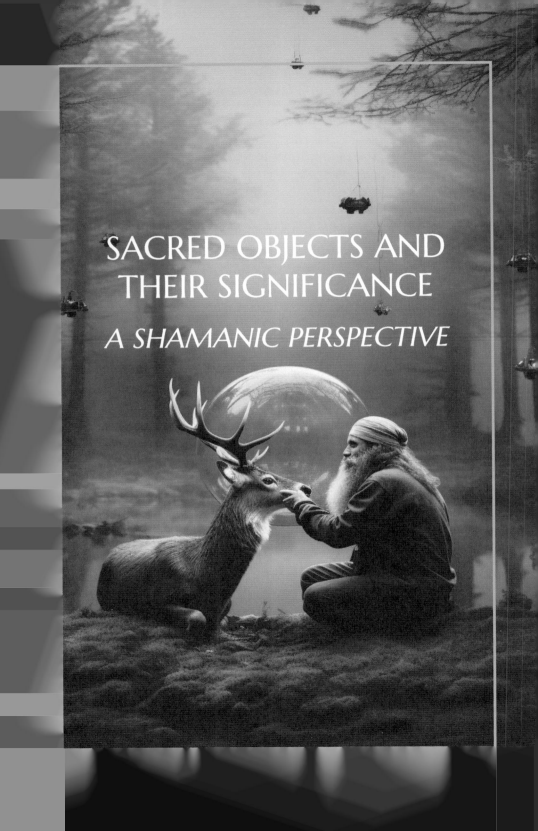

SACRED OBJECTS AND THEIR SIGNIFICANCE

A SHAMANIC PERSPECTIVE

"A shamanic perspective"

From a Shamanic practitioner's viewpoint, sacred objects form a vital bridge between the seen and the unseen world. They're not inanimate objects, but embodiments of spirit energies, ancestral connections, elemental essence, and personal intent.

Each object within a Shamanic practitioner's sacred space holds a specific purpose and energy resembling forces found in nature or representing ancestral wisdom.

For instance, a practitioner may use a drum or a rattle, traditional tools symbolic of the heartbeat of Mother Earth and used to connect with the spirit world during rituals.

Symbols of faith may include figurines or symbols relating to spirit animals or sacred ancestral symbols. Personal memorabilia could represent the practitioner's lineage or past lives, serving as powerful reminders of ancestral wisdom.

In Shamanic practice, stones and crystals aren't just chosen for their aesthetic appeal, but for the unique and potent energies they're believed to hold. The selection of these can greatly vary depending on the practitioner's purpose, spiritual connection or guidance received from the spirit world.

Incorporating elements like candles or oil lamps resonates with the element of fire, driving away negative energy, and representing spiritual enlightenment. The use of incense mirrors the spirit of air, carrying prayers and intentions to the spirit world.

For a Shamanic practitioner, a dedicated journal might contain records of dream interpretations, spirit journeys or divination readings. Similarly, tools like wind chimes, bells, or singing bowls may not just signify the beginning or end of a ritual, but *are used to clear energy and create vibrational doorways into the spirit world.*

Thus, from a Shamanic viewpoint, the sacred objects in the sanctuary are embodiments of living energies, each with a purpose and role to play, transforming the sacred space into a vibrant and sentient spiritual realm.

CHAPTER 6

TECHNIQUES TO MAINTAIN THE SACREDNESS OF YOUR SPACE

reating your sacred space is only the initial crux of the journey. Equally essential is the maintenance and preservation of its sanctity, ensuring it remains a fertile ground for self-care activities, personal growth, and spiritual exploration. This process requires consistent attention and care, similar to tending a flourishing garden.

Here are some techniques on how to preserve and nourish the sanctity of your sacred space:

1. Regular Cleaning and Decluttering:

Like any other part of your home, your sacred space demands regular cleaning. However, in this case, cleaning is not just a routine task but becomes a mindful ritual ensuring the energy of the sanctuary remains clear. Keeping your sacred space clutter-free is equally vital as clutter can cloud the mind and hamper focus.

2. Energetic Cleansing:

Beyond physical cleanliness, your space may need energetic decluttering too, especially after intense healing or spiritual work. This could be done using numerous techniques like burning sage or Palo Santo sticks, use of salt lamps or crystal grids, or chanting cleansing mantras.

3. Frequent Engagement and Practice:

Perhaps the most effective way to maintain the sanctity is by engaging with your space daily. Regular engagement can be anything from sitting quietly, meditating, journaling, yoga, or any other practice that brings peace and calm. This regular engagement imprints positive and healing vibrations into the room, keeping its sacred essence alive.

4. Reassess Regularly:

Over time, as we grow and evolve, so may the significance of the objects in our sacred space. Frequently reassess your sanctuary to ensure everything within it still holds meaning and resonates with your current state of mind and spiritual journey.

5. Mindful Entrance and Exit:

Before entering your sacred space, take a moment to mentally prepare yourself. Similarly, when leaving, take a few moments to express gratitude for the peace and insights your space provides.

Remember, the preservation of your sacred space is a testament to the respect and reverence you have for your well-being and personal growth journey. Up next, we will dive into how to use your sanctuary effectively for self-care and personal growth-promoting activities, exploring the manifold avenues these sacred spaces can open in your journey towards self-discovery, healing, and evolution.

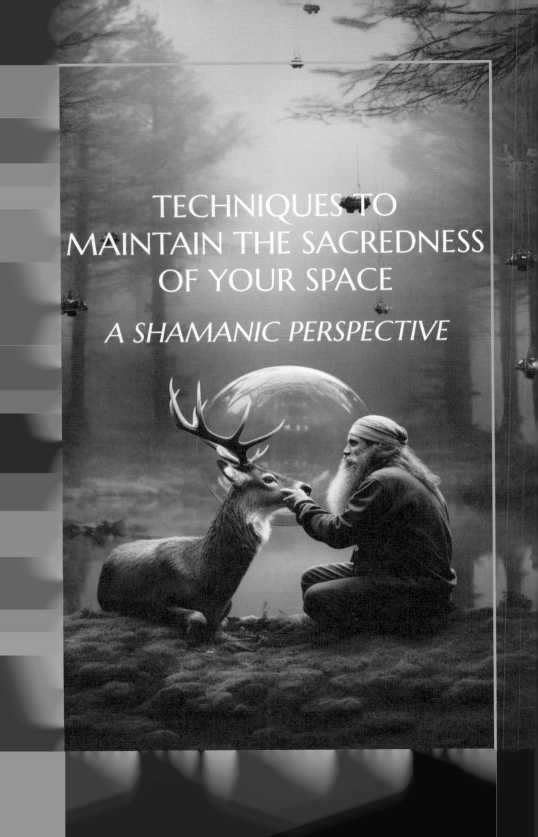

TECHNIQUES TO MAINTAIN THE SACREDNESS OF YOUR SPACE

A SHAMANIC PERSPECTIVE

"A shamanic perspective"

For Shamanic practitioners, maintaining the sacredness of a space entails energetic harmonization with nature's rhythms and vigilant purification to ensure an unhindered connection with the spirit world.

Cleansing plays a significant role in a Shamanic approach to maintaining sacredness. They might use ritualistic smudging with sage, palo santo, or other herbs to drive away negative energies and invite positivity. The act of lighting these sacred herbs represents the unity of the four elements—earth (herb), fire (flame), air (smoke), and water (resin)—making it a ritualistic practice to cleanse and balance the energy within the space. The act of drumming or the ringing of a bell can serve as an energy cleanser, purifying the space and making it reverberate with harmonious frequencies.

Harmonizing their space with the rhythms of nature, like moon cycles or seasonal changes, is vital for a Shamanic practitioner. They consider the natural rhythms in their rituals and decor, such as incorporating seasonal plants or aligning rituals according to moon phases, amplifying the connection with the cosmic order.

Invoking spirit guides, ancestors, or elemental spirits forms an integral part of their practice, inviting them to protect, guide and bless their sacred sanctum. By incorporating this into their routine, they ensure a continuous flow of positive energy and spiritual connectivity. Thus, to a Shamanic practitioner, maintaining sacredness is about ensuring the sacred space is energetically cleansed and aligns with natural and spiritual forces consistently. This maintenance ritualistically reinforces the sanctity of the space, creating a thriving nexus between the physical and the spirit realms.

CHAPTER 7

HOW TO USE YOUR SPACE FOR PERSONAL GROWTH ACTIVITIES

Once you've established and are maintaining your sacred space, the real transformative journey begins. Utilize your space effectively to drive self-care practices and personal growth activities that speak to your heart. The serenity of your sanctuary acts as fertile ground for the seeds of personal growth to germinate and flourish.

Below are some suggestions on how you can effectively engage with your sacred space to facilitate self-care and personal development:

1. Meditation and Mindfulness:

With the tranquility of your sacred space as a backdrop, you can practice regular meditation or mindfulness exercises. These practices reduce stress, enhance attention, improve emotional well-being, and foster deeper self-relations.

Example: Set a daily alarm at a convenient time and sit in your sacred space for a guided meditation. It can be a simple mindfulness exercise like observing your breath or doing a body scan meditation.

2. Yoga or Physical Movements:

Yoga or other mindful movements not only promote physical well-being but also mental clarity, awareness, and spiritual growth. Your sacred space can provide a serene environment conducive to these practices.

Example: You may start with a simple "Sun Salutation" sequence in the morning. As your practice deepens, incorporate more complex asanas or create your own flows optimized for your physical and mental wellbeing.

3. Journaling:

Journaling can be a powerful tool for self-discovery and psychological healing. The quietude of your sacred space serves as the perfect setting to explore your thoughts and emotions through writing.

> **Example:** Start with a "stream of consciousness" journaling, where you write whatever thoughts flow into your mind. Later, you can introduce specific themes like gratitude journaling, dream journaling, or even letter-writing to your future or past self.

4. Reading:

Keeping a selection of inspiring books in your sacred space aids your personal growth journey. The peaceful environment lets you absorb and reflect on the wisdom at your own pace.

> **Example:** Choose a book that focuses on personal growth or philosophy. Spend a dedicated time each day in your sacred space reading and writing down insights or reflections in a separate notebook.

5. Breathing Exercises:

Practices like pranayama or other breathing exercises can help reduce anxiety, improve focus, and cultivate a deep sense of calmness. Performing these in your sanctuary can strengthen their effects.

> **Example:** Begin with simple exercises like "Box Breathing" or "4-7-8 breathing". As you build capacity, explore more adventurous practices such as alternate nostril breathing or Wim Hof's breathing method.

6. Expressing Gratitude:

A sanctuary can serve as a special spot to acknowledge your blessings and express gratitude. This practice nurtures an optimistic worldview and enhances overall life satisfaction.

Example: Maintain a gratitude journal within your sacred space and make a routine to note down at least three things you're grateful for, each day.

7. Affirmations or Visualization:

Your sacred space can act as a force multiplier when practicing affirmations or visualizations. These practices can increase self-belief, trigger positive changes, and steer you towards your goals.

Example: Use affirmative statements that resonate with your personal goals, and voice them out loud in your sanctuary, perhaps in front of a mirror. For visualization, harness your imagination to mentally rehearse your goals, letting the peaceful energy of your space amplify these images.

8. Self-reflection:

Take the time to reflect on your past experiences, current realities, and future aspirations. The tranquility of your sacred space can allow you to gain deeper insights into your lives.

Example: Carve out time each week to reflect on your actions, decisions, and emotions. Ask fundamental questions like, "What made me happy this week?" or "What challenged me, and how did I react?". This puts you in a pattern of constructive introspection.

9. Therapies:

If you are into sound therapy, Reiki, or other forms of holistic therapies, a sanctuary is a perfect place to perform.

Example: If you practice sound therapy, place your singing bowls, chimes, or any other instruments in your sacred space. For Reiki or similar holistic practices, conduct your sessions in your sanctuary with its added tranquillity.

All these actions taken in your sacred space will gradually weave into your daily or weekly routine, leading you to uphold a balanced and mindful life. The next chapter invites you to discover the profound effects a sacred space can have on your spiritual life. Let's delve into exploring this connection.

HOW TO USE YOUR SPACE FOR PERSONAL GROWTH ACTIVITIES

A *SHAMANIC PERSPECTIVE*

"A shamanic perspective"

The Shamanic practitioner views the elements of self-care as a harmonization of the energies within the self and the environment. Using their sacred space for personal growth activities is a key approach to bridge mind, body, and spirit, and to nurture a deeper relationship with the natural and spirit world.

Reveling in silence within this sanctuary could mean meditative journeys to discover one's spirit animal or connect with spiritual guides. Reading in solitude might involve not just inspirational books but scripts of ancestral knowledge or mythologies to understand hidden wisdom.

Personal growth manifests in practicing rituals, like creating an altar, invoking the four directions, or drumming. Many Shamanic practitioners engage in sacred dance, expressing their internal emotions and honoring their connection with Nature and Spirit. Artistic self-expression in a Shamanic practitioner's sacred space could include crafting their own talismans, painting spirit visions, or writing inspired by their journeys. Engaging in such activities strengthens their understanding of self and their connections with the cosmos.

Physical fitness practices might echo natural cycles and might include yoga flows that mirror the strength and fluidity of different animals, or breathwork practices inspired by the wind's rhythm. Such a Shamanic perspective on self-care promotes a balance between physical, mental, emotional, and spiritual realms. In essence, from a Shamanic practitioner's perspective, the sacred space serves as a spiritual gymnasium of sorts – a place where they nurture their instinctual wisdom, enhance their spiritual connectivity, and integrate personal growth into all facets of their being.

CHAPTER 8

SPIRITUAL CONNECTION & SPIRITUAL PRACTICE IN YOUR SACRED SPACE

At the very heart of every sacred space is a powerful nexus that connects the physical realm with the spiritual. It is this connection that blesses this hallowed environment with the transformative power to cultivate spiritual habits, expand consciousness, and foster profound mystical experiences.

Whether your spiritual inclination leans towards religious practices, esoteric philosophies, or artistic expression, your sacred space can serve as a special place for these deeply introspective and personally enriching activities.

Here is how you can effectively utilize your sacred space to nourish and deepen your spiritual connection:

1. Spiritual Practices:

Sacred spaces can act as the perfect setting for spiritual practices like prayer, meditation, energy work, yoga, tantra, or Zen arts. The psycho-spiritual ambiance of your space uplifts the efficacy of these practices and grounds you in the present moment.

2. Connection to Higher Consciousness:

Your sacred space can serve as a gateway to higher dimensions of consciousness. Through meditative or trance states, chants, mantras, or divination tools, you can transcend the physical plane to gain spiritual insights or divine communication.

3. Creating Rituals:

Rituals hold immense significance in spiritual traditions. They provide structure and foster deeper connections with divine forces. Lighting a candle, burning incense, practicing breath work, or creating an altar are all examples of rituals that can be personalized to your beliefs and incorporated into your routine.

4. Reflection and Introspection:

Your sacred space is a secure and serene environment conducive to introspection. Regular self-reflection can lead to spiritual revelations, a greater understanding of your divine purpose, and discovery of your true self.

5. Expressing Gratitude:

Expressing gratitude is a powerful spiritual exercise, as it reconnects us with the abundance of life and fosters a more profound appreciation for the cosmic scheme of things. Cultivating a habit of expressing gratitude in your sacred space helps instill an optimistic outlook and a happier mindset.

6. Sacred Study:

Whether it's religious text, spiritual literature, philosophical discourses, or mystic poetry, sacred space can be a serene spot for such studies. Spiritual reading in the tranquility of your sanctuary can help enrich and deepen your spiritual understanding and growth.

7. Mindful Creativity:

Many people find a spiritual connection through artistic expression. Paint, sketch, write, or make music. Engaging your creative side in this nurturing environment not only fosters self-expression but also facilitates spiritual healing and growth.

As we journey deeper into our inner selves within our sacred spaces, we unlock doors of understanding that help us connect more deeply with the world around us and build stronger bonds with our spiritual understanding. A sacred space, therefore, not only provides us with a retreat but also propels us towards spiritual advancement and mindful living.

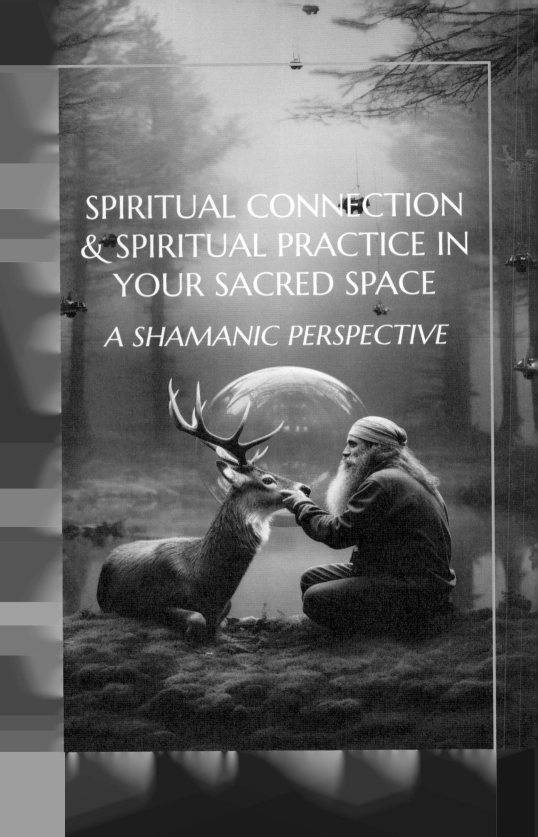

SPIRITUAL CONNECTION & SPIRITUAL PRACTICE IN YOUR SACRED SPACE

A SHAMANIC PERSPECTIVE

"A shamanic perspective"

In the Shamanic tradition, the sacred space serves as a vibrant interface between the physical world and the spirit realm. A Shamanic practitioner sees their sacred space as a spiritual antenna, amplifying their receptivity to divine wisdom and guidance.

Establishing a spiritual connection within this space often involves animistic beliefs, where each element holds a spirit, a life force. From the gentle sway of a feather to the resonating hum of a crystal or the flicker of a candle flame, everything embodies a dialogue with the spirit world.

The approach to spiritual practices varies - some may use divination tools like tarot cards, others might practice journeying drum sessions, and some might engage in ritualistic dances or chants for a spiritual connection. A Shamanic practitioner may engage in silent listening, inviting guidance from ancestral spirits, nature spirits, or power animals. They could meditate, seeking to dissolve the boundaries between the self and the cosmos, or save a corner for honoring their ancestors, igniting a deep spiritual connection with their lineage.

The invocation of elemental spirits forms a key part of their spiritual practice, keeping the sacred space buzzing with elemental energies. In essence, a Shamanic practitioner's dedicated sacred space surpasses the physical realm, serving as a medium for communicating with the spiritual world. The spiritual practices within this space, thus, foster a profound, transforming connection with the great web of existence.

CHAPTER 9

SACRED SPACES ACROSS
CULTURES: LESSONS AND
INSPIRATIONS

The concept of a sacred space weaves itself into different cultures and spiritual practices across the globe, often reflecting remarkable commonalities as well as fascinating distinctions. These spaces, albeit with different names and rituals, share the collective aim of nurturing peace, promoting spiritual growth and grounding individuals in self-awareness. Each has a story to tell, culture to represent, and wisdom to impart.

By looking into the diverse realm of cultural respect to the sacred, we can draw a plethora of inspirations and lessons to enrich our own personal sanctuaries.

1. Japanese Zen Gardens:

Japan's Zen Buddhism philosophy manifests strikingly in their rock and gravel-filled Zen Gardens. These spaces symbolize serenity, evoking a sense of harmony and uncluttered thinking. Creating a miniature Zen Garden in your sacred space could bring a profound air of tranquility and mindfulness.

2. Native American Medicine Wheel:

Used in Native American spiritual practices, a Medicine Wheel symbolizes the cosmos and the individual's journey within it. The addition of a medicine wheel in your sacred space could serve as a spiritual tool or a piece of art symbolizing unity and sacredness.

3. Indian Mandir:

In Indian households, a Mandir or a prayer room provides a sacred space for meditation, prayer, and spiritual connection. Incorporating elements from this cultural space may involve setting up a small altar with deities, symbols, or photographs relevant to your spiritual beliefs.

4. Moroccan Riads:

Riads, traditional Moroccan styled houses built around an interior courtyard, exhibit how open-air spaces can be transformed into a quiet retreat and a connection with nature. Adding elements of Riads to your space might set a soothing background chorus of birds humming, water fountains trickling, or wind chimes subtly clinking.

5. African Ancestor Altars:

In African cultures, Ancestor Altars are constructed as a site of reverence for ancestors. Setting up an ancestor altar with photographs, heirlooms, or candles can keep you connected with your heritage and ancestors.

6. Orthodox Icon Corner:

In Orthodox Christian practice, an Icon Corner serves as a personal chapel within a home. Icons (religious art) are arranged to orient the individual in prayer. A personal "Icon Corner" in modern context might consist of inspirational pictures or symbols guiding your spiritual practice.

SACRED SPACES ACROSS CULTURES: LESSONS AND INSPIRATIONS

A SHAMANIC PERSPECTIVE

"A shamanic perspective"

From the Shamanic practitioner's perspective, sacred spaces across various cultures present a rich tapestry of interconnections with the Earth, elements, spirits, and ancestors. These universal themes resonate deeply with the Shamanic view, presenting lessons and inspirations that can further enrich their own practices.

Across many cultures, sacred spaces might be geographical locations, physical structures, or personal altars. In Shamanic practice, each of these carry significance as potential gateways to the spirit realm, endowed with power and significance by faith, intent, and rituals. Inspiration comes in observing the shared practice of incorporating elements of nature into sacred spaces across cultures. Whether it's the use of water in Hindu temples, incense in a Buddhist shrine, or the concept of sacred Cardinal Directions in Native American cultures, they all mirror Shamanic elements.

There are lessons, too, in the diversity yet unity of values across cultures. While practices vary, there's a shared reverence for sacred spaces as places of healing, growth, and a bridge to the ethereal realm. The portable sacred spaces seen in nomadic traditions or the intricate sacred geometries used in constructing divine structures in some cultures provide further inspiration - one emphasizes the fluidity of sacred spaces, and the other, their energetic resonance.

Hence, the multiplicity and richness of sacred spaces across cultures offer valuable insights and affirm the universal pursuit of spiritual growth, connection, healing, and transformation. These serve as inspirations, broadening the ontological understanding for a Shamanic practitioner, inviting them to weave these enriching threads into their own sacred space tapestry.

CHAPTER 10

CHALLENGES IN MAINTAINING SACRED SPACES AND HOW TO OVERCOME THEM

Just as the journey of personal growth encounters roadblocks from time to time, maintaining a sacred space can also present its sets of challenges. Identifying these challenges and coming up with effective solutions is pivotal to relishing the tranquility and purpose the space is designed to offer.

Challenge 1: Clutter Accumulation

Over time, the added items, both intentional and unintentional, can accumulate into clutter, which may diminish the tranquility of the space.

> *Solution:* Schedule a regular maintenance session. Once a week or bi-monthly, ensure to declutter, dust off, and re-organize your space. It's also beneficial to clear out unnecessary objects or those which no longer resonate with your current state of mind.

Challenge 2: Balancing Privacy and Household Demands

In bustling households, maintaining privacy for your sacred space can be challenging, with interruptions from kids, pets, or even everyday chores.

> *Solution:* Set clear boundaries and rules about your sacred space with your family members. If it's plausible, use a room divider or curtain for added privacy. Well-defined time slots for your quiet contemplation can also mitigate interruptions.

Challenge 3: Consistently Engaging with the Space

Maintaining a consistent practice, be it meditation, gratitude, or journaling in the sacred space can become challenging with demanding schedules or lack of motivation.

> *Solution:* Integrate your time in the sacred space into your daily routine. A dedicated slot, be it the morning or

before bedtime, helps establish consistency. Remember, even a few minutes spent can positively influence your day and outlook.

Challenge 4: The Space Evolving with Your Growth

As we progress on our spiritual or personal growth journey, the sacred space may become stagnant and cease to align with our evolved needs and preferences.

Solution: Regular reassessment of your space is vital. Consider if the objects and setup still reflect your energies and aspirations. Don't hesitate to innovate, modify, or reestablish your sanctuary as needed.

Remember, facing challenges is a part of every journey and holds the potential for immense growth. In the next chapter, we will discuss how to let your sacred space evolve over time, aligning it with your ongoing journey of personal and spiritual growth.

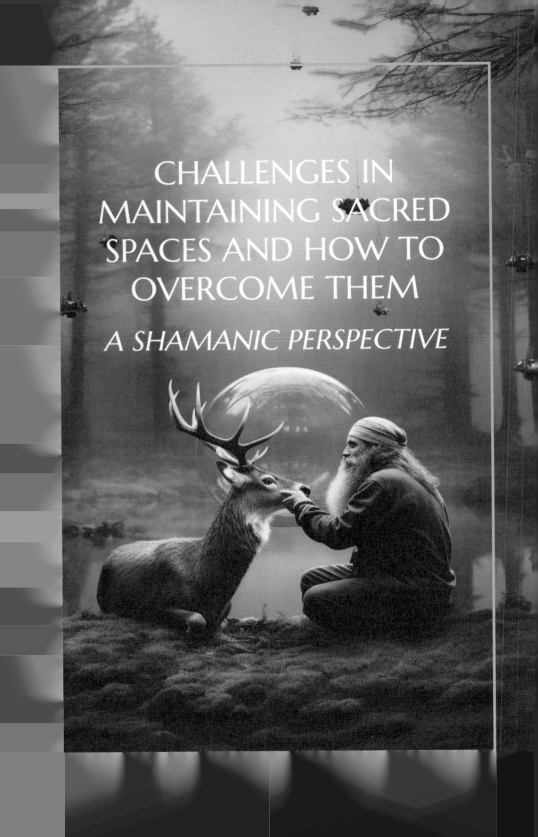

CHALLENGES IN MAINTAINING SACRED SPACES AND HOW TO OVERCOME THEM

A SHAMANIC PERSPECTIVE

"A shamanic perspective"

From the Shamanic practitioner's viewpoint, maintaining a sacred space entails walking a spiritual path with its inherent challenges and triumphs.

One common challenge could be the space's disruption by others or everyday life interruptions. In Shamanic practice, the key here is the understanding that the sacredness of space comes not just from its physical attributes but also the practitioner's intent. The resilience to recreate the sacredness anywhere, even within imperfections, is what makes the sacred spaces truly personal and private.

Maintaining consistency of spiritual practices within the space can also be a challenge. For a Shamanic practitioner, this may mean persisting with daily rituals, connecting with spirit guides, or performing cleansing ceremonies, even in times of spiritual dryness. A community of fellow practitioners or supportive people can help to overcome this challenge, providing motivation and collective energy.

Distractions, be they internal or external, can be another tough hurdle. The Shamanic practitioner might overcome this by incorporating calming elements in their sacred space, like soothing sounds or comforting scents, which help quiet the mind and center focus on the spirit's pathway.

Lastly, some could struggle over the feeling of inadequacy as though their sacred space or practice is not "good enough." Here, the Shamanic perspective emphasizes that each sacred space is a unique and authentic reflection of the individual's spirit journey, not a race for perfection.

CHAPTER 11

EVOLVING YOUR SACRED SPACE: ADAPTING TO LIFE'S SHIFTS

Part of the deep beauty of our journeys is that they're in a constant state of flux, pulsating with growth and transformation. As we evolve, our needs, preferences, and aspirations rhythmically shift and expand, demanding that our physical environments align with these dynamic changes. This principle wholeheartedly applies to our sacred spaces too.

Learning to adeptly navigate these waters and allowing our sacred spaces to gracefully evolve with us enhances their significance, utility, and ability to support our journey of growth and self-discovery.

Here are some pointers on how to let your sacred space evolve along with your personal trajectory:

1. Stay Tuned In and Receptive:

Listen to the subtle (or loud) whispers of change from within. Stay receptive to the evolving needs of your spiritual or self-care practices, and the elements or layout that no longer serve you.

Example: Over time, you might feel that your morning yoga routine has now shifted to evening or that your once preferred silence is now replaced by soothing instrumental music. Listening to these subtle changes helps in realigning your sacred space to your current preferences.

2. Harness the Power of Reinvention:

From repositioning the furniture to updating the color scheme, or even transitioning a corner into an indoor garden, get creative with reinventing your space to resonate with you better.

Example: Perhaps your cozy corner by the window, with a comfortable chair and a stack of books, has now evolved into needing a larger space for your newly discovered passion in art therapy. Consider repurposing a less-used part of your living room into an art corner.

3. Adapt to Life Changes:

The arrival of a new family member, a shift to a new location, or even a change in career paths, might necessitate you to rethink your sacred space. Try to adapt to these life changes with flexibility and creativity.

> **Example:** If you're moving to a house with limited space, consider creating a portable sacred space — where your spiritual objects are housed in a beautiful box that you can unpack anytime you want to engage with your practices.

4. Add Mementos from Life's Milestones:

Incorporating objects or symbols that signify personal milestones, like a token from a transformative trip or a book that shifted your perspective, keep the space in tune with your personal growth.

> **Example:** Perhaps you completed a significant project at work that challenged and helped grow your skills. Celebrate this by placing the acknowledgment certificate or a token representing this achievement in your sacred space.

5. Upgrade Your Tools and Aids:

Based on your growth in spiritual practices or mindfulness techniques, it might serve to upgrade or add new tools, like a more complex meditation cushion, sound bolsters for sound therapy, or advanced yoga props.

> **Example:** Maybe your mindfulness practices have deepened, and you want to explore advanced meditation techniques. You could add a new meditation timer or an app

subscription that provides guided meditations for more profound practices.

6. Seek Inspirations:

From nature, travels, books, or even social media platforms – remain open to inspirations. They can encourage you to add new elements to your space or fresh perspectives for its evolution.

> **Example:** You might visit a botanical garden and fall in love with the tranquil vibe of the plants. This could inspire you to add more indoor plants to your sacred space, enhancing the serenity through nature's essence.

Embracing the evolution of your sacred space channels the unfolding of your personal journey into a physical form, enhancing the sacred space's value in nurturing your well-being and personal growth. As we end our comprehensive guide on sacred spaces, in the next and final chapter, we motivate you to spread the tranquillity and self-awareness by promoting the idea of sacred spaces among your loved ones.

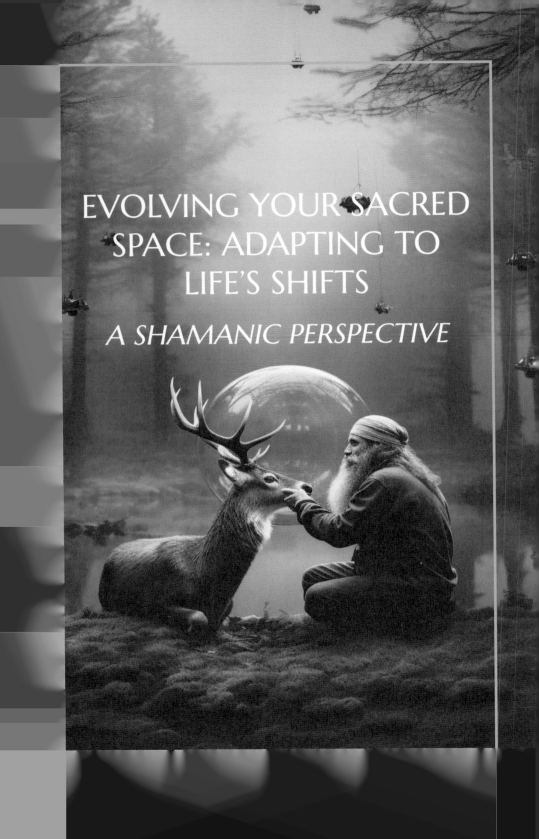

EVOLVING YOUR SACRED SPACE: ADAPTING TO LIFE'S SHIFTS

A SHAMANIC PERSPECTIVE

"A shamanic perspective"

In the Shamanic viewpoint, life's shifts and changes are considered a natural part of our spiritual journey, and the sacred space should ideally echo these transformations. It's viewed not as a static entity but a living and evolving sanctuary reflecting the phases, growth, and transformations of one's spiritual life.

Adapting to life's shifts might involve remodeling the sacred space to reflect changing spiritual aspirations or personal life transitions. For example, the coming of a new season could be marked by incorporating elements that mirror the season's spirit.

A Shamanic practitioner might view major life changes as times to reconfigure the energy or focus of their sacred space. Significant events, like a birth or death in the family or a major personal accomplishment, can be acknowledged through changes like adding or removing objects that represent these shifts in the sacred space.

Should a Shamanic practitioner experience a shift in their spiritual journey—perhaps a new spirit guide or a novel insight from a spiritual quest, it would likely lead to an evolution of their sacred space too. It might involve adding symbols, amulets, or colors that connect them better to their new spiritual phase.

In circumstances of physical relocation, the Shamanic practitioner sees it as an opportunity to reestablish their sacred space harmoniously with the new environment. They would likely seek to build a spiritual and energetic connection with the new location, inviting local spirits and elementals to their new sacred sanctuary.

Therefore, Shamanic practitioners perceive the evolution of their sacred space as necessary, welcoming, and symbolic of their own personal and spiritual growth. It's the reflection of their dynamic bond with the spirit world and their path in the physical world, where change is the only constant.

CHAPTER 12

SACRED SPACE ON THE GO: NURTURING SPIRITUALITY WHILE TRAVELING

We often view travel as a welcome break from our daily routines, an excursion into new experiences, and a way to broaden our perspectives. However, maintaining the continuity of our spiritual practice during travels can seem challenging. Moving across time zones, adjusting to new schedules and environments, and the lack of a personal sacred space can potentially disrupt our spiritual routines.

Yet, with a little bit of creative thinking and commitment, we can ensure that our spiritual practices remain undisturbed even when we're on the move. Let's explore ways in which we can create a portable sacred space that accompanies us wherever our journey takes us.

1. Portable Sacred Objects:

Carry along mini-versions of your sacred objects such as miniature idols, a compact version of your favorite spiritual book, or even a small vial of calming essential oil. A mini-altar kit could consist of small artifacts nestled in a beautiful, compact box that encapsulates the spirit of your sacred space. This portable collection of your spiritual aides can keep you anchored to your practices even when you're miles away from your home sanctuary.

2. Technology to the Rescue:

In an era where technology has seamlessly blended with our lives, let it aid your spiritual journey as well. You can download meditation apps which offer a range of guided meditations. Apps specific to journaling, mandala creation, or even healing sound baths can be handy. Carry your spiritual reading material as ebooks or audiobooks. Digital platforms can be transformative in maintaining your spiritual routine during travel.

3. Leveraging Natural Surroundings:

Mother Nature offers sanctuaries in abundance. Depending on where you travel, attune with the available natural elements. If you're near a water body, embrace the calming energy of water in your spiritual practice. In the mountains, let your spirits soar high with the peaks. In an urban setting, a city park can become your oasis of tranquility. By attuning yourself to nature's rhythm, you not only maintain your spiritual practices but also enhance them with newfound experiences.

4. Hotel Room Sanctuary:

Your temporary dwelling can very well house a temporary sacred space. Identify a quiet corner or a portion of the room where you feel most comfortable. Arrange your portable sacred objects, perhaps even adding a local floral touch, and voila, you have a sacred haven set up. Whether it's a low-light corner for meditation or by the window for morning yoga, this space can fuel your spiritual practice.

5. Mindful Activities:

Mindful activities such as meditative walking, doodling, journaling, or even washing dishes can be powerful spiritual practices requiring no specific setup. The key is to be fully present in such activities, savoring the experience, and letting it offer mental clarity and relaxation just as your regular spiritual practice would.

6. Visualization:

Lastly, but certainly not least, mastering the art of visualization can dramatically assist in maintaining spiritual continuity. When sitting down for meditation or reflection, picture your home sacred space. Imagine the familiar objects, the positioning, the associated scents, or sounds, and recreate the experience in your mind. This psychological tool can harness your subconscious and create an effective spiritual session, minus any physical setup.

These versatile strategies ensure that travel doesn't disrupt your spiritual practice. Instead, travel opens up avenues for innovative adaptations and enhances spiritual learning experiences, inculcating a deeper sense of adaptability and flexibility in your spiritual journey.

SACRED SPACE ON THE GO: NURTURING SPIRITUALITY WHILE TRAVELING

A SHAMANIC PERSPECTIVE

"A shamanic perspective"

For Shamanic practitioners, the idea of carrying their sacred spaces with them while traveling resonates deeply. The sacred space is seen less as a place and more as an extension of one's spiritual self. This view allows for the portability and adaptability of the sacred space to various environments.

Traveling might prompt a Shamanic practitioner to create a mobile sacred space kit—small and portable yet potent in invoking the spiritual realm. They could consider including small items like the four elements symbols, a miniature drum, spirit animal amulets, ancestral tokens, or divination cards.

Meditation or connection with the spirit world can be practiced in transient places— hotel rooms, airports, or even out in nature. A simple act such as drawing a circle or setting up a small corner with symbolic objects could serve to momentarily shift an everyday place into a sacred space, aligning to the Shaman's spiritual need.

Connecting with a new location from a Shamanic perspective might involve establishing a dialogue with the local spirits of the land, water bodies, or natural landmarks. Reaching out to these spirits could offer a sense of spiritual grounding in unfamiliar or temporary spaces. It's a practice that underlines the Shamanic belief of interconnectedness with all living things, wherever they may be.

Thus, the concept of "sacred spaces on the go" aligns with the Shamanic understanding of spirituality as pervasive and adaptable. It confirms that the sacred space is not simply a physical area but encapsulates the interplay between the practitioner's intent, the spiritual realm, and the chosen environment.

CHAPTER 13

PASSING THE LEGACY

The transformative power of maintaining a sacred space is an experience to be shared. Encouraging loved ones to create their own sanctuaries not only offers them a tool for self-exploration and personal growth but also strengthens the bond between you, nurturing shared experiences and discussions.

Here are some ways you can inspire others to create their sacred spaces:

1. Share Your Experience:

Talk about your journey and how having a sacred space has influenced your life. You could share before and after experiences, specific personal growth instances, or even challenges that you overcame.

> **Example:** Narrate to a friend how meditation in your sacred space has positively impacted your emotional wellbeing by using personal anecdotes. For instance, detail the time you successfully navigated a stressful situation at work by applying mindfulness techniques honed in your sanctuary.

2. Gifting Meaningful Objects:

Consider gifting them a unique spiritual or mindful object to spark their interest. It could be a beautifully crafted journal, a set of beginner's meditation cushions, or a soothing indoor plant. These thoughtful gifts could form the foundation of their own sacred space.

> **Example:** Gift a loved one a beautiful indoor friendly fern, a reminder of nature's tranquility, and a starting point for creating their space. Or a handcrafted journal with an inspirational quote on its cover might encourage them to make note of their thoughts and reflections in their newly formed sacred space.

3. Invite Them Over:

If they're comfortable, invite them to experience your sacred space firsthand, creating an opportunity for them to feel the calmness and positive energy that a well-tended sacred space can radiate.

> **Example:** Plan a small tea ceremony within your sacred space and invite a close friend over. During the visit, let them experience the peace and tranquility of your haven. Share the various components of your sacred space and how each one has a specific role in your spiritual practice.

4. Share This Guide:

Invite others to purchase, or gift this comprehensive guide. It could be a valuable resource that answers their queries, provides practical tips, and stimulates their thoughts on creating a meaningful sacred space.

> **Example:** Recommend this guide to a friend who's expressed interest in personal growth. Better still, gift them a physical copy if available, marking pages or sections you found particularly insightful. Emphasize how the guide has been a resource in assisting you, providing practical tips and stimulating thoughts on creating a meaningful sacred space.

5. Nurture Their Journey:

Be supportive as they embark on this journey. Encourage them to personalize their space and remind them that it's not about perfection but a reflection of their individuality and spiritual journey.

> **Example:** As your friends embark on their own journey of creating a sacred space, offer thoughtful insights while reaffirming the importance of personalization. Remind them

that their sacred space is a reflection of their individual tastes, affinities, and spiritual inclinations and does not need to be perfect in any other perceptions but theirs.

Remember, every seed you plant in inspiring others to create a sacred space, you are essentially proliferating pockets of peace, personal growth, and mindfulness in various corners of the world.

PASSING THE LEGACY

A SHAMANIC PERSPECTIVE

"A shamanic perspective"

Guiding others to establish their sacred space from a Shamanic practitioner's perspective involves imparting knowledge about the interconnectedness of all life, the significance of the natural elements, and the possibility of an intimate relationship with the spirit world.

Encouraging others to build their own sacred space, a Shamanic practitioner would emphasize creating a space that resonates with their personal spiritual journey.

They might instruct them on ways to invite the elemental forces into their space, possibly through symbols, objects, or ritual practices.

A Shamanic practitioner might inspire others by sharing personal experiences of feeling centered, guided, and spiritually enriched through their own sacred space. They would lay emphasis on the sacred space as an individualized spiritual hub, where one might communicate with one's spirit guides, practice self-care, or carry out intuitive development activities.

They might guide others on the importance of maintaining their sacred spaces too—through energetic cleansing rituals, rhythmic alignment with nature, and the regular invitation of spirit guides. This fosters the space's resonance with the individual's evolving spiritual journey.

Furthermore, teaching others to stay open to their space's evolution—adapting it in response to personal growth or changes in their spiritual path, could form part of passing this Shamanic legacy.

From a Shamanic standpoint, encouraging others to create their sacred spaces is akin to empowering them to forge stronger spiritual connections and self- understanding. It's about passing on, not just the physical practice of creating a sacred space, but the profound associated spiritual wisdom and perspective.

CONCLUSION – ILLUMINATING PATHS THROUGH SACRED SPACES

In essence, a sacred space, be it a quiet room bathed in the warm glow of the rising sun, a peaceful corner adorned with tokens of personal victories, or a tranquil patch of greenery rustling softly in the evening breeze, serves as more than just a physical location. It manifests as an intimate, living memoir of your journey towards peace, self-discovery, and personal growth.

This guide has aimed to lead you, step-by-step, through this captivating journey of creating, maintaining, and evolving your sacred spaces. From the initial stone we cast onto the calm waters of conceptualizing such a space, triggering ripples of considerations to take into account, to the gentle yet transformative waves of understanding the cultural diversities, challenges, and the innate need for such spaces to grow with us - we've traversed an enlightening path.

May the practical steps and spiritual philosophies entwined within the chapters of this guide serve as a beacon to illuminate your path. As you imbibe the wisdom held within these pages and implement them, allow your sacred space to transform into a nurturing soil for the seeds of introspective practices such as meditation, gratitude declaration, journaling, conscious movement, or simply being.

It is my sincere hope that these practices, stoked and amplified by the sanctity of your personal enclave, cascade into your daily life, leaving trails of tranquility, mindfulness, and heightened self-awareness.

As you revel in the serenity of your sacred space and embark on personal and spiritual growth paths, we encourage you to become conduits of this profound wisdom. Inspire others to create their sanctuaries and watch as these individual islands of peace stitch a soft, almost imperceptible connection; a private yet shared bond that meanders across hearts and homes, bridging us in ways that echo of shared aspirations, collective spiritual progress, and unwavering respect for individual journeys.

Upon this concluding note, I end this comprehensive guide but not without wishing you an eventful journey. A journey marked by introspective silences, enlightening eurekas, ardent self-improvements, and, most crucially, an ever-evolving sacred space that faithfully mirrors your indomitable spirit's untiring evolution.

As I sign off, here's an inspiring thought to reverberate within your sacred space and beyond: Each of us has the potential to be architects of peace, mindfulness, and purpose, first within our souls and then in the world. Armed with this knowledge and a sacred space to bolster it, may we all pledge to undertake this transformative journey and leave an indelible imprint of love and meaning in the sands of time and spirit,

Angell Deer

The Sacred Web

Uncover the profound transformation that waits within the intimate wilderness of your personal sanctuary, as you journey through "The Sacred Web: The magical craft of Your Sacred Shamanic Space".

Diving into the heart of Shamanic wisdom, this guide walks with you as you design, tend, and evolve your sacred spaces, resonating with your unique spiritual journey.

Discover the essence of a sacred Shamanic space, see how it serves as more than a mere physical area and evolves as a living embodiment of your spiritual passage. The book navigates everything from choosing your spot, decorating with elemental force symbols, to the significance of different sacred objects within your sanctuary.

Learn to maintain the sacredness of your space, overcoming challenges that arise and adapting it to life's inevitable shifts. Explore how your sacred space can nourish personal growth and deepen your connectivity with the spiritual realm.

Draw inspiration from sacred spaces across various cultures and receive valuable guidance on nurturing your spirituality, even while on the go. Emergent as an influential feature of this book is the encouragement it provides to pass on the legacy, empowering others to create their own sacred spaces.

"The Sacred Web: The magical craft of Your Sacred Shamanic Space" acts as your companion into the spiritual exploration of your own being, encouraging you to strengthen your bond with Nature, Spirits, Ancestors and your Inner Landscape. Hold the keys to your spiritual sanctuary, and unlock a new resonance within your home, your life, your spirit, and the cosmos.

Printed in Great Britain
by Amazon

44383476R00050